TEN ONE-ACT PLAYS

OTHER BOOKS BY CRANE JOHNSON

Past Sixty

The Wither'd Garland

Seven Short Plays

Seven Strange Plays

Tiger In Crystal (With Gerald Ball)

Seven Shorter Plays

Twenty-Five One Act Plays

ALSO

Jack and the Beanstalk (A children's play with music)

TEN ONE ACT PLAYS

by
CRANE JOHNSON

MIDDLEBURY COLLEGE
LIBRARY

THEATRE PRESS
550 Fifth Avenue
New York 36, N.Y.

TEN ONE ACT PLAYS
Copyright © 1967, by
CRANE JOHNSON

All Rights Reserved

PS
3560
0374 T4

Library of Congress Catalog Card No. 67-28842

PRINTED IN UNITED STATES OF AMERICA BY
Theo. Gaus' Sons, Inc., BROOKLYN 1, N.Y.

CONTENTS

THE VERY SUPERIOR CLERK

All rights, including professional, amateur, motion pictures, recitation, public reading, radio broadcasting, television, and the rights of translation into foreign languages are strictly reserved. All inquiries are to be directed to Crane Johnson, in care of Theatre Press, 550 Fifth Avenue, New York, New York 10036.

THE VERY SUPERIOR CLERK

THE CLERK
THE SUPERIOR, An imagination

Place: A cheap hotel room

Time: The present

THE VERY SUPERIOR CLERK

(The scene is a table and chair in a cheap hotel room. The Clerk, a small, insignificant creature, is pouring himself a drink)

CLERK: (*Matter-of-factly*) Free. Forty years I worked for him. But now I am free.

SUPERIOR: (*Offstage*) Free. (*Throughout the play the voice permeates the stage. Or, if the director prefers, the Superior could be behind a screen on stage, or in a pool of light apart from the Clerk. Or the Superior could move about the stage, not being noticed directly by the Clerk. Stage movements are indicated in the event the latter choice is selected*)

CLERK: (*Gesturing hand to audience*) That's him. My superior. For forty years my superior. But no longer. I am free.

SUPERIOR: (*Coming out onto stage*) Free.

CLERK: Every morning at nine I went in and sharpened his pencils.

SUPERIOR: I liked them sharp.

CLERK: I put all the little objects on his desk in order.

SUPERIOR: I like my things in order.

CLERK: I was as good as he was. (*Explaining to audience*) It was just circumstances that I was his clerk. (*Pours drink into glass*) Good as he was. Good as he *is*. (*Swallows liquor*) Now I can tell him. It's come to an end. Retired. That's what I am. Free. Free, that's what I am. Free.

SUPERIOR: Free. (*The Clerk rises*)

CLERK: Yes. Free! Free! Free! (*He leaves the table, crosses left, and stands apart from the table*)

SUPERIOR: Free.

CLERK: No more to stand before you bowing. (*Bows*) *All men are equal.* (*Clasps hands behind back*) No more will I stand before you bowing and waiting to hear of your need.

8

SUPERIOR: My need.

CLERK: Smiling with servility because that is what you liked, but hating you. Knowing I was more than just a menial. I was a good clerk.

SUPERIOR: That is true.

CLERK: (*Shaking hand*) You will not find another so easily. That's what I say to you, that's what I say. Not so easy to find someone to sharpen your pencils and put things just so. (*Shakes both hands in front of him*) I wasn't an *ordinary clerk*.

SUPERIOR: You were useful to me. Another will have to be ordered.

CLERK: (*Gesturing with hand*) Ho ho! You may think it's that easy. (*Returns to behind desk and pantomimes action to describe next line*) It won't be easy to find a clerk who'll sharpen your pencils the way I did and arrange things on your desk. *All men are equal.* I'm as good as you. I knew that all along. (*Sitting*) If only circumstances had been different.

SUPERIOR: What circumstances?

CLERK: (*Struggling for an idea*) . . . Education.

SUPERIOR: You could have taken night courses.

CLERK: There never was time. I was always so tired evenings.

SUPERIOR: Yes, the work . . . the work . . . the sharpening of my pencils and the arrangement of the things on my desk.

CLERK: You never found fault . . . you can't say you ever found fault.

SUPERIOR: (*After pause*) I never noticed. One cannot notice everything. Most of what one finds around oneself is insignificant. (*Crossing over*) You were that. Insignificant.

CLERK: You won't find a clerk so easily to replace me. I'm retired. (*Rising triumphantly*) Free. That's what I am. Free. (*Throws arm out*)

SUPERIOR: Free for what.

CLERK: (*Terrified*) For what!

SUPERIOR: (*Contemptuously*) Yes, free for what. What will you do. What can you do. Now retired. Now equal. Free to equal your petty insignificance with those other petty insignificants.

9

CLERK: (*Stepping out right of table*) You can't talk to me that way. I don't have to listen any more. I don't have to listen to you *any more.*

SUPERIOR: Then, goodbye...

CLERK: (*Right arm out and terrified*) No, don't go. (*Pleading with single hand*) Speak. (*Both hands pleading*) Please, speak.

SUPERIOR: I don't speak. I only order.

CLERK: (*Crossing to back of chair*) No more! (*Grabbing back of chair with both hands*) You order no more!

SUPERIOR: Goodbye.

CLERK: (*Right hand out*) No, don't go. (*Both hands on back of chair*) I must tell you what I think. Of my hatred for you. These forty years.

SUPERIOR: I shall remain.

CLERK: I must tell you my true thoughts. (*Sits at table*) When I sharpened those pencils year after year. Arranging the things on your desk, knowing I was just as good as you. (*Bringing hands together*) Oh, I dreamed of this day, the day I would bring it all to an end. (*Hands to chest*) Be free.

SUPERIOR: Now you are free.

CLERK: Free! Free! Free! (*Holds hands to chest*)

SUPERIOR: (*After pause*) Free for what?

CLERK: (*Terrified*) You can't talk to me like this. (*Spreading hands on table*) Not now. Now that I am free.

SUPERIOR: Free for what, Mr.... Mr.... I don't believe I caught your name.

CLERK: (*Leaving hands on table*) I worked for you forty years. I sharpened your pencils and arranged the things on your desk.

SUPERIOR: Do you have a name.

CLERK: (*Folding hands on table*) I am I. And you must realize that! And I am free.

SUPERIOR: Goodbye.

CLERK: (*Opening palms of hands slowly*) No, not yet. Not until I've told you...

SUPERIOR: I'm waiting.

CLERK: (*Further opening of palms*) What I plan to do.

SUPERIOR: (*Crossing over to table*) And what, *whatever your name is*, do you plan to do. (*Pause*) Now that you are free.

CLERK: (*Remaining in same position, but not believing his statements*) I shall . . . I shall . . . I shall be free.

SUPERIOR: I'm waiting.

CLERK: (*Same mood*) Free, that's what I shall be . . . (*Palms of hands down on table top*) . . . Free.

SUPERIOR: To do what!

CLERK: (*Rising triumphantly*) To sharpen my own pencils, that's what! (*Great laughter from Superior*)

CLERK: (*Smiling*) Yes, now that I am free I shall sharpen my own pencils.

SUPERIOR: And who will there be to notice. No one.

CLERK: I'll find a friend.

SUPERIOR: *I* was never your friend.

CLERK: That is true. You only looked to see if the pencils were sharp.

SUPERIOR: You were good at that.

CLERK: (*Leaning over desk, arms out, and speaking excitedly*) You admit that. You admit that.

SUPERIOR: (*Crossing right*) Yes, I admit that.

CLERK: It won't be easy to find a replacement. (*Pantomime of desk action again*) One to sharpen your pencils and arrange the things on your desk and to smile servilely and walk softly out of the room.

SUPERIOR: I shall push a buzzer and there will be a replacement.

CLERK: (*In slight panic, clenching fists and bringing them to chin*) No, No, not that way. (*Drops both arms to side in pleading position*) Not so easily. (*Bringing both hands up slightly*) And why didn't you ever ask me my name.

SUPERIOR: There was no reason. You were so insignificant.

CLERK: You never complained. (*Gesturing to table*) About the pencils. You never complained.

SUPERIOR: That is true. (*Stepping two steps right*) Goodbye.

11

CLERK: (*With slight hand gesture*) No, don't go. (*Turning slightly to left*) You pretend it isn't important. That you'll find it easy to replace me now that I am free.

SUPERIOR: A minor inconvenience of pushing the buzzer for your replacement.

CLERK: But only *I* know how you like the points.

SUPERIOR: You are free now. Retired.

CLERK: (*Proudly*) By choice. The law didn't force me. (*Steps left away from table*) I could have gone on. For five more years. (*Crosses arms in front*) But I chose to be free.

SUPERIOR: You chose to be free. Goodbye.

CLERK: (*Throwing arms down angrily and turning in direction of Superior*) Who is he? Who took my job.

SUPERIOR: He will come in tomorrow and sharpen the pencils and arrange my desk. I probably won't even look up or ask his name.

CLERK: (*Hands still down*) But that's my job. (*Pointing to desk*) He has no right to touch your pencils with his dirty hands. (*Keeps finger out*)

SUPERIOR: But now you are free.

CLERK: No right. (*Brings back hand and states matter-of-factly*) That is *my* job. (*Proudly*) Only *I* know how they are to be sharpened. (*Pointing*) How *you* like *your* things on the desk.

SUPERIOR: Goodbye, whatever your name is.

CLERK: (*Drops hands to low pleading position*) Please, don't go. There's noone here.

SUPERIOR: Now you are free.

CLERK: I don't know what to do. I've not been prepared.

SUPERIOR: Goodbye.

CLERK: Why did you throw me out. (*Drops arms to side and doesn't really believe his next speech*) I'm as good as you. Why did you throw me out.

SUPERIOR: You chose retirement. Freedom.

CLERK: (*Hands still down*) A trick. Someone wanted my position. (*Vigor restored*) Now I know. (*Waltzing a bit*) I'm not stupid. (*Waltzing some more*) I'm clever. I could go to the law.

12

SUPERIOR: For what.

CLERK: (*Proudly with both hands in air*) My position!

SUPERIOR: Goodbye. (*Clerk goes down on knees*)

CLERK: For God's sake!

SUPERIOR: Goodbye.

CLERK: No.

SUPERIOR: (*After a long pause, going over to Clerk and circling him*) Until the morning. Tomorrow morning. At nine. And don't be late. I don't like tardiness.

CLERK: (*Hands on knees*) Never late, Sir. I was never late.

SUPERIOR: That is true. (*Crossing right*) And now goodbye. Until tomorrow. (*Clerk looks up happily with tears running down his face and leans back on his knees*)

CLERK: (*Hands to each side*) God bless you, Sir.

(*The lights dim out and the curtains close*)

END

THE OLD LADY DECIDES TO DIE

All rights, including professional, amateur, motion pictures, recitation, public reading, radio broadcasting, television, and the rights of translation into foreign languages are strictly reserved. All inquiries are to be directed to Crane Johnson, in care of Theatre Press, 550 Fifth Avenue, New York, New York 10036.

THE OLD LADY DECIDES
TO DIE

CHARACTERS

THE OLD LADY
ANDROMACHE
THE PRIEST AND ATTENDANTS

Setting: Florence

Time: The past

THE OLD LADY DECIDES TO DIE

(Before the curtains part we hear soft crying of a woman's voice. When the curtains part, we see the bedroom of the Old Lady. She is in bed, propped up by large pillows. The bed is down center stage with its head portion elevated several feet for audience visibility. Near the Old Lady, but apart, stands her old servant Andromache who holds a handkerchief up to her nose and is weeping. A priest and his attendants are ceremoniously leaving the room. They've just given last rites to the Old Lady. After they've gone, the Old Lady speaks)

OLD LADY: I'm glad I was born a Catholic. I've always loved pageantry and theatricals. Always loved a good show. The blazing gold and crimson red. The high-flung banners. The flickering candles. And best of all I've liked the last rites. The hushed atmosphere and the open weeping. Yes, I've always liked a good performance of the last rites. *(Andromache cries aloud)*

OLD LADY: Oh, for heaven's sake, Andromache, stop that blubbering. One hundred years is a nice round number. It is about time I decided to die. Yes, about time. And now that I've decided to die you'll be free of me. You and that rascal man of yours can go back to Rome and set up a small business of some kind. You'll have the money—with what I'm leaving you together with all your pilfering through the years. *(Andromache steps forward and puts up her hand)*

OLD LADY: Oh, it doesn't matter. I've deducted it from the amount I've left you. *(Pause)* Oh, what a good feeling it is. Now that I've made the decision. Now that I have decided to die. Nature has been kind. Has allowed me to live long enough to find all this living "stale, flat and unprofitable." *(To Andromache)* That is a line from a play. I once played Hamlet. Once knew all the lines. All. But this phrase is all I remember. "Stale, flat and unprofitable." Bring me my jewel box, Andromache. (*Andromache gets the jewel box from a locked drawer which she opens with a key. She hands it reverently to the Old Lady. The Old Lady opens the lid*)

OLD LADY: Oh what treasures this box once contained. Rubies, diamonds, emeralds, pearls. Tributes to my youth, my talent, my beauty. Long, long ago. (*Pulling out items*) Now, only trinkets, junk. To be yours soon, Andromache. When I am finally dead.

ANDROMACHE: Oh, thank you, Madame.

OLD LADY: You'd have filched them anyway. So I am easing your conscience. The little you may have left. (*Andromache turns away*)

OLD LADY: You've had a good life with me, Andromache. An easy life. I've paid you well and you've met interesting people. You've met the many who've come to me as a pilgrimage. Come to kneel beside my bed. The reverent, the devout . . . the curious.

ANDROMACHE: Oh, yes, Madame, there have been so many.

OLD LADY: A legend in her lifetime. Coming to look. Coming to stare at the mistress of Italy's greatest playwright, *Carlos di Salvatore.* (*Andromache gasps*)

OLD LADY: There, I've said it. For the first time in fifty years. The mistress of Carlos di Salvatore. *That is the legend.* Always whispered. Never confirmed. The legend which sets *you* apart, Andromache. The legend which you repeat to all your servant friends and which they in turn repeat to their ladies. I, the mistress of Carlos di Salvatore. I the one who spent a glorious summer with him at Ravenna on the Adriatic and who changed his whole style of writing. *That is the legend.* I who inspired his last and greatest play . . . And when I am finally dead a newspaper will offer you money to tell of my last moments. And you, in a way, my dear Andromache, will also become part of the legend. A stupid, common old woman, but faithful to the last, will become part of the legend. You will be faithful, won't you, Andromache?

19

ANDROMACHE: Oh, yes, Madame.

OLD LADY: Will you be faithful even after, Andromache? Even after I die?

ANDROMACHE: Oh, yes, Madame.

OLD LADY: Bring the books, Andromache, and read the passages to me. The same passages you read to me every night. However tonight will be the last time. For tonight I have decided to die. (*Andromache sniffles a bit, brushes her nose with a handkerchief and goes over to a chest upon which there are several books and brings them back*)

OLD LADY: Begin, Andromache. (*Andromache has placed books on table near bed. She picks up one which has a marker, opens it, and begins to read*)

ANDROMACHE: Carlos di Salvatore continues to be Italy's most talented and mysterious playwright. For twelve years he wrote poetic tragedies which marked his genius, then just before his death, he wrote his first and only comedy in a style that was so different, so fresh, that a whole new career was predictable. What brought about the change? Perhaps the famous actress, still living, who was near him that summer in Ravenna. It is thought they met first at the Tomb of Dante—both carrying slim volumes of his verse.

OLD LADY: (*Interrupting*) The Tomb of Dante. Do you know, Andromache, that there was a feud—for years—between Florence and Ravenna over who was to have Dante's bones. Finally, Pope Leo the Tenth, a Medici, gave them to Florence. When they opened the coffin ... all they found was a "fragment of bone and a few withered leaves of the laurel which had adorned the poet's head."

ANDROMACHE: (*Continuing her reading*) But in the autumn his tragic death was to occur and that actress remains alive, sad, and silent.

OLD LADY: After his death I wore black. Always black. For fifty years I wore black.

ANDROMACHE: (*Picking up another book and reading*) The only explanation for the complete change in view and style of Carlos di Salvatore was that in the adjoining room of that

20

small hotel in Ravenna was a beautiful, vibrant actress who, immediately upon his death, wore only black. Her suffering has become an international legend. She has acted only in *his* plays, the tragedies only. Never in his last play—the comedy.

OLD LADY: They never mention my name. Never. But everyone knows. I looked good in black.

ANDROMACHE: (*Reading still another book*) It is reported they first met in the pinewoods outside the city. Walked hand-in-hand where Byron walked.

OLD LADY: (*Interrupting*) ... "in the solitude
Of the pine forest, and the silent shore
Which bounds Ravenna's immemorial wood,
Rooted where once the Adrian wave flowed o'er."

(*To Andromache*) Lord Byron lived eighteen months in Ravenna. Because of the Countess Guicciolli.

ANDROMACHE: (*Continuing her reading*) Will the silent lady who lived in the room next to Carlos di Salvatore that summer in Ravenna ever speak. Ever help to explain the sudden change. The joy in his new writing. Were there letters before his sudden tragic death?

OLD LADY: (*Waving hand*) Enough. Hand me my jewel box again, Andromache. (*Andromache does so*)

OLD LADY: (*Pushing a button and watching a drawer open*) You see, Andromache, there was a secret drawer. (*Andromache looks astounded*)

OLD LADY: Surprised, eh? All these years and you didn't know. (*Takes out a folded letter*) No jewels, but something more precious. A letter from Carlos di Salvatore. The only letter he ever wrote me.

ANDROMACHE: (*Eagerly*) Oh, Madame.

OLD LADY: Bring a candle near, Andromache. (*Andromache does so*)

ANDROMACHE: Imagine! A letter from Carlos di Salvatore!

OLD LADY: I read it from time to time. Now this is to be the last time.

ANDROMACHE: A letter from Carlos di Salvatore!

OLD LADY: You have pledged fidelity, yes, Andromache?

ANDROMACHE: Oh, yes, Madame.

OLD LADY: Even after death.

ANDROMACHE: Oh yes, Madame.

OLD LADY: It is only rarely that one may become a legend in one's own lifetime. A legend. A legend. Dante. Lord Byron. The Countess Guiccioli. Carlos di Salvatore. And I. I, I, I. Part of the great legend of Ravenna. Ravenna. Ravenna. Ravenna. I have enjoyed it. The legend. Being part of it. There has been no loneliness because ... of the legend. Many have come ... almost as a pilgrimage.

ANDROMACHE: Oh, yes, Madame, there have been so many.

OLD LADY: (*Handing letter to Andromache*) Read the letter ... The last part only. But first, light all the candles. All. Let the room blaze in light. (*Andromache eagerly lights all the candles about the room and then returns to side of the Old Lady*)

OLD LADY: Now read. The last part only.

ANDROMACHE: (*Reading*) "I write with some concern, since we met only once and then only casually." (*To the Old Lady*) Oh, what a firm hand he had.

OLD LADY: (*Commanding*) Read.

ANDROMACHE: (*Reading*) "I have learned upon my return to Florence that you are given as the reason for my so-called change in style." (*To the Old Lady*) A firm hand but with a flourish.

OLD LADY: (*Infuriated*) Read.

ANDROMACHE: (*Reading*) "I hope that if our accidental meeting in Ravenna has resulted in bringing you embarrassment because of the rumors linking us you will silence them with a pronouncement, even stating if you desire that my joy of this past summer has been because of my love for a young lady sojourning at a nearby villa. My love is secret but the world will soon know her name. Yours truly, Carlos di Salvatore."

OLD LADY: *Carlos di Salvatore.*

ANDROMACHE: (*Aghast*) Then ... it's not true. It's never been true. For fifty years ...

OLD LADY: An imposter! For fifty years an imposter.

ANDROMACHE: Oh, Madame! (*Andromache stands and holds her face in hands, sobbing. This is the greatest blow of her life*)

OLD LADY: (*After a very long pause*) Give me the letter, Andromache. (*Andromache does so*) Now, hand me the candle. No. not that one. The silver one. (*Andromache hands the Old Lady the candle. The Old Lady begins burning the letter*)

OLD LADY: Cremation by silver and flame. (*When the letter is aflame she puts it on a dish and watches until the letter is in ashes*)

OLD LADY: You will be faithful, Andromache.

ANDROMACHE: (*Still sobbing*) Yes, Madame, I will be faithful.

OLD LADY: Faithful to the legend. That's all I ask of you. To be faithful. Beyond my death.

ANDROMACHE: Yes, Madame, beyond death.

OLD LADY: You have been a good servant, Andromache. Dear, old, ancient, Andromache. Now, go, and let me die. (*Andromache slowly leaves the room. When she is gone, the Old Lady closes her eyes, slowly pulls the sheet up over her face, and dies as the curtains slowly close*)

END

THE INHERITANCE

All rights, including professional, amateur, motion pictures, recitation, public reading, radio broadcasting, television, and the rights of translation into foreign languages are strictly reserved. All inquiries are to be directed to Crane Johnson, in care of Theatre Press, 550 Fifth Avenue, New York, New York 10036.

THE INHERITANCE

CHARACTERS

JOHN
HENRY
LIVINGSTON

Setting: Empty room in mansion

Time: The present

THE INHERITANCE

(John and Henry enter the large empty room of a mansion. It has the air of not having been lived in for many years)

JOHN: Room after room. Empty. Corridor after corridor. Empty. The dust. The stale air. The gloom. The emptiness. The magnificent emptiness.

HENRY: Not lived in for twenty years. *(John wanders over to the huge magnificently carved fireplace)*

HENRY: One can almost imagine Uncle Charles living here. Entertaining his friends. The long banquet table piled high with food. The silver gleaming. The crystal sparkling. The candles flickering. One can almost imagine that these walls have absorbed some of the qualities of the generations of people who lived and visited here. Now gone. Ghosts, all of them.

JOHN: *(Noticing buttons beside fireplace)* What beautiful ivory buttons.

HENRY: They rang the servants' quarters. *(John pushes merrily and turns away)*

HENRY: Uncle Charles lived in a period when all was order and all was predictable. He awoke each morning to a world familiar to him. Knowing *it* and his particular place and position in it.

JOHN: Oh, to have been alive then instead of now, eh? God, to have been alive then!

HENRY: A world which still believed in concepts. Living concepts such as . . . *loyalty* and *duty*. They weren't just words soon to wear out and be tossed aside.

JOHN: Will you sell the place?

HENRY: Who would buy it? All these empty, empty rooms. Poor Uncle Charles. He thought he was leaving me an inheritance. *(A door slowly opens and Livingston walks in. He is a very old man in livery. He squints in direction of Henry who is closest to him)*

LIVINGSTON: You rang, sir? I thought you'd forgotten me. It's been over twenty years. *(Both John and Henry look at Livingston in amazement as the curtains close)*

END

THE CHURCH TEA

All rights, including professional, amateur, motion pictures, recitation, public reading, radio broadcasting, television, and the rights of translation into foreign languages are strictly reserved. All inquiries are to be directed to Crane Johnson, in care of Theatre Press, 550 Fifth Avenue, New York, New York 10036.

THE CHURCH TEA

CHARACTERS

MRS. ADAMS
MRS. BROWN
MRS. CHARLES

Setting: Home of Mrs. Adams

Time: The present

THE CHURCH TEA

(The scene is the home of Mrs. Adams. Mrs. Adams sits behind a tea table with a memo in her hand. To each side of her are the other ladies, sitting and sipping tea)

MRS. ADAMS: *(Consulting memo)* And that event will be followed by Brotherhood Week. Now what activities could the church promote for Brotherhood Week? *(Both women think as they sip their tea)*

MRS. ADAMS: We might each of us invite a Negro into our home. *(Both women nod in agreement and continue to sip their tea)*

MRS. BROWN: *(After a moment)* I don't know any Negroes.

MRS. CHARLES: Nor do I.

MRS. BROWN: How does one meet them? *(Mrs. Adams looks at her memo again and the two other ladies continue to sip their tea thoughtfully)*

MRS. ADAMS: And that is followed by Cancer Detection Week.

MRS. BROWN: Perhaps a film. The ladies always love films.

MRS. CHARLES: Oh, yes, a film! *(Mrs. Adams consults her memo again as the other two ladies continue to sip their tea)*

END

34

CONFLAGRATION AT KICKAPOO

All rights, including professional, amateur, motion pictures, recitation, public reading, radio broadcasting, television, and the rights of translation into foreign languages are strictly reserved. All inquiries are to be directed to Crane Johnson, in care of Theatre Press, 550 Fifth Avenue, New York, New York 10036.

CONFLAGRATION AT KICKAPOO

CHARACTERS

BOB ADAMS

HARRY KOSZAK

PROFESSOR J. HEFFNER DOODLE

P. COLON CREEKBOTTOM

MARTIN LUTHER HUXLEY

MISS GERALDINE SNOOKER

EUSTACE TERWILLIGER

JONES

HARGRAVES

Setting: Interior of a Shill Service Station

Time: A past period of peace and innocence

CONFLAGRATION AT KICKAPOO

(*The scene is the interior of a Shill gasoline service station in a small American town. Off right, down stage, is a doorway leading to the outside. Upstage from this doorway is a stand which houses the cash drawer. Next to this stand are new or old tires. Against the back wall, right, there is a doorway with the sign "Gents" hanging above it. Center upstage against back wall is a display rack containing cans of oil, etc. Next to this, up stage left, is another doorway with the sign "Ladies" hanging above it. On the left side of the set are found more tires, etc., and downstage a desk, cluttered, next to an open door which leads to the lubrication room. On the wall left there is a pay telephone which is between desk and left corner of the room. After the curtains have parted for a moment, Bob Adams enters, greatly excited. BOB ADAMS is still in his teens, a rather artistic looking fellow who looks out of place in the gas attendant togs he wears. Bob dashes towards the phone, is about to take down the earpiece, when he suddenly remembers his greasy hands. He picks up a rag off the desk and begins wiping his hands, rather gingerly at first, but then roughly. He then goes back to telephone, starts to dial, then remembers he needs a coin. He looks through pockets, does not find the right coin, dashes over to the cash drawer right, opens it, takes out a coin, starts towards telephone again, is about to use it, when he decides to leave I.O.U. note in drawer. This he writes at desk, dashes over to cash drawer again, deposits note, returns to telephone and begins to dial. Halfway through he stops, hangs up quickly, and consults telephone directory. When he's found the correct number, he dials quickly and then waits excitedly for an answer which finally comes*)

ADAMS: Hello, Profesor Doodle? Oh, Mrs. Scratchly, I didn't recognize your voice. Do you have a cold? Yes, please, I want to speak to Professor J. Heffner Doodle. (*Waits*) Hello, Professor Doodle? I hope I didn't call you away from anything important. This is Bob Adams, Adams, you know, one of your art students. Yeah, I'm in your History and Appreciation of Art Culture, 293, meeting at 10 on Mondays, Wednesdays, and Fridays. But, of course, you'd know the hours. Anyway, something terrific just happened to me and I think you should know about it. I work Saturdays at the Shill service station and we get all kinds of people here, being as this is the main highway from New York to San Francisco. Oh, I'm sorry, Professor Doodle, do you think your bath water will get cold? Well, what I wanted to say is that guess who just went through after stopping for gas and oil? Give up? None other than *Guido Eniro*. (*Waits*) That's right. Guido Eniro, the great Italian painter. I knew that'd floor you. I recognized him right away. He's on his way to San Francisco in a big car with a chauffeur and everything. Yeah, I wish you could have met him, too. Oh, he's short, very Italian looking and doesn't look at all like he'd painted at the Vatican. I only talked to him for a minute but I told him our art professor, Mr. J. Heffner Doodle, that's you, considered him the greatest living painter and that before long people would be building shrines to him. You said that in last Monday's lecture. Do you remember, Professor Doodle? (*Harry Koszak enters from right. KOSZAK is a nondescript, ignorant man in his forties who is lessee of the station from the Shill Oil Company. Koszak throws an angry glance at Adams at the phone, then enters through the door marked "Gents." Adams, realizing he'd better get back on the job, turns hastily to phone again*) Well, I gotta hang up now, Professor Doodle. I'll see you in class Monday and maybe I should make a special report or something. Yes, goodbye, Professor, have a nice bath. (*Adams hangs up the receiver rather dreamily and just stands there by the phone looking out into space. A moment passes and Koszak comes out of the Gents room raging mad*)

KOSZAK: That dirty, low-down...

ADAMS: What's the matter, Mr. Koszak?

KOSZAK: Here I get the station all ready for the monthly inspection what those company officials is making this afternoon and what happens!

ADAMS: The plumbing's out again?

KOSZAK: Worse!

ADAMS: The cockroaches are back?

KOSZAK: You remember that little dark fellow, the dumb screwy-looking one?

ADAMS: You mean Mr. Eniro.

KOSZAK: Whatever his name is, he went into the (*pointing*) can and drew pictures all over the walls.

ADAMS: (*Dumbfounded*) Guido Eniro ... drew pictures on the walls?

KOSZAK: Yeah, and not in pencil either. I don't know what he used, but they won't come off with soap and water.

ADAMS: *Guido Eniro.* And he gets over $100,000 a picture. *Guido Eniro.*

KOSZAK: The inspectors are due here in half an hour. I got marked down last month because they found some spark plugs in the carbuerator box. And now today, when they find this! (*Koszak storms angrily off into the Lube room. As soon as he's gone, Adams picks up the phone again, and repeats the actions that opened the play. Finally, he reaches someone on the other end*)

ADAMS: (*Excitedly*) Hello, Professor Doodle? Oh, hello, Mrs. Scratchly. I hope your cold's better. You haven't a cold? I wonder if I could speak to Professor Doodle. Oh. Well, could you have him come out. I'm sure he won't mind when he hears what I've got to tell him. (*Waits*) Hello, Professor Doodle? This is Bob Adams again, I'm in your History and Appreciation of ... Oh, you remember? That's nice. A lot of professors don't even seem to want to remember ... what, no, that's not why I called you. Were you enjoying your bath? That's good. I hope the water doesn't go cold, but what I wanted to say is about Guido Eniro. Well, not only was he here, but he's drawn paintings all over one of our walls here. Yeah, a sort of mural, I guess. Mr. Koszak just discovered them. Yeah, can you imagine. Here at Kickapoo, of all places. We're the only ones in America who have examples of his work. It'll put Kickapoo on the map, won't it, Professor Doodle, and your History and Appreciation of Art Cul-

40

ture can make field trips here. (*Adams' attention is interrupted by Koszak who enters from left carrying a large bucket of paint and some brushes. When he reaches the door marked "Gents" Adam hangs up and screams out*)

ADAMS: Mr. Koszak, what are you doing?

KOSZAK: Nothing to do but paint over them gol-blasted drawings before the company inspectors come.

ADAMS: Paint over ... paint over *Guido Eniro?*

KOSZAK: I don't know or care who that guy was. I'm tired of getting it in the neck from those inspectors. Today we're going to pass that inspection perfect.

ADAMS: But you can't, Mr. Koszak. Guido Eniro is one of the world's greatest painters. Maybe the greatest. His works are in Rome at the Vatican.

KOSZAK: They may be O.K. at the Vatican wherever that is, but they ain't O.K. in Harry Koszak's Shill Service Station and out they go, with this heavy duty paint. I've got two brushes, so come in and help me before them officials arrive.

ADAMS: But, Mr. Koszak, you can't, it'd be sacrilegious.

KOSZAK: Oh, it would, would it. We'll see! (*Koszak begins to enter when there's a honk outside*)

KOSZAK: Catch that customer while I take care of this.

ADAMS: It's Mr. Hooper. He always likes you to wait on him.

KOSZAK: Damn that Hooper! (*Turning*) Well, you git started while I gits Hooper filled and gone. (*Koszak exits. Adams waits until he's gone, then returns to telephone, dashes over to cash box, is about to repeat earlier ritual, when he decides to just pick up cash drawer and take it over to telephone with him. This he does, deposits coin, dials, and soon has a party on the line*)

ADAMS: Oh, Hello, Mrs. Scratchly, your cold is getting worse. Oh, it's you, Professor Doodle. How was your bath? Oh, you haven't taken it. You're catching pneumonia instead. That's nice. I mean, oh, Professor Doodle, the most awful thing is about to happen! Just because there's a company inspection in about fifteen minutes, Koszak insists we paint over Guido Eniro. Yeah, oh, it does no good. He doesn't know anything about art and you know how dumb these big oil company officials are. And they don't care anything about art, just more money. What? You'll be right down. I'll hold him off if I can. How soon can you be here? Your car's broken down? Gee, that's awful. Mrs. Scratchly's son Jim used to have a bicycle, maybe you could borrow that. Yes, but hurry, please 'cause I'm sure Mr. Koszak will outtalk me and I'll be painting out that mural. (*Koszak rushes in, grabs a can of oil*)

KOSZAK: Of all days, his car would need oil. Why aren't you in there painting! (*Koszak rushes out right. Adams picks up another coin from cash drawer, looks up a number hurriedly*)

ADAMS: Hello, Miss Geraldine Snooker. Oh, well, who is this? Mr. Eustace Terwilliger, her lawyer. Oh, hello, Mr. Terwilliger, this is Bob Adams, remember me. My father hired you to defend me the time I broke Mrs. Jones' window. Yeah, Robert Adams. Oh, I'm fine, and how are you? Is Miss Snooker there? Well, it's rather personal. Oh, hello, Miss Geraldine Snooker. This is Robert Adams. Adams. I used to mow your lawn. Four summers ago when John Harris had the infetigo and couldn't go out. Yeah, that's me. Well, anyway, Miss Snooker, I read all about you from time to time in the papers and know how much you're interested in art. Well, you'd be interested in knowing that Guido Eniro the greatest artist of our time just went through Kickapoo. That's right. Yeah, I'm sorry you didn't get to meet him. I just didn't think about it at the time. I hope you're not angry. No, but he did some mural work here at the service station where I work. Koszak's Shill Service on Main Street just three blocks north of the post office. But something awful will happen to those murals if you don't come down right away. (*Sees Koszak coming*) I gotta hang up now, Miss Snooker. Please come down 'cause if you don't the world of art will have lost a rare work all because of you. That'd be an awful thing for the world to say about you, wouldn't it. Goodbye! (*Koszak reenters, goes for the cash drawer, sees its absence, looks towards Adams who sheepishly carries the drawer across right and places it in cabinet. Koszak puts money in box, silently goes over, picks up*

42

paint, beckons to Adams, and is about to turn again, when in through lube entrance comes Professor J. Heffner Doodle on an ancient bicycle. DOODLE is in his late fifties, a bewildered man generally except when he has a burning purpose. Doodle is dressed in a flaming, multi-colored bathrobe. He jumps off his bicycle and runs, placing himself between Koszak and the wall)

DOODLE: Stop! This is infamy! Put down that paint!

ADAMS: Professor Doodle!

KOSZAK: Say, who's this? Some guy out of the nut house?

ADAMS: This is Mr. Doodle, Mr. Koszak. Professor J. Heffner Doodle who teaches the art courses at Kickapoo U.

KOSZAK: Well, tell him to scram. We've got work to do.

DOODLE: Over my dead body, sir. *(To Adams)* I came as quickly as I could. No time to dress. That can come later. History is at stake, my boy. I called Mr. Creekbottom, our president, and he's rushing down also.

ADAMS: Gee, not P. Colon Creekbottom himself?

DOODLE: The same.

KOSZAK: Look, professor, I don't know what this is all about, but there's gonna be an inspection this afternoon. In about ten minutes, in fact. I may lose my job if they find . . .

DOODLE: And what about your soul? Would you worry as much about losing that?

KOSZAK: My soul? What's that to do with this?

DOODLE: Everything. Why, Mr. . . . .

ADAMS: Koszak. K-O-S-Z-A-K.

DOODLE: Do you realize, Mr. Koszak, that you have on your walls here the only specimen in America of work done by the one, the only, Guido Eniro, undoubtedly the greatest spiritual painter of our age, whose works hang in the Vatican.

KOSZAK: Look, I ain't got nothing against art, I ain't mad at nobody or nothing, see, I just gotta pass that inspection.

DOODLE. These inspectors, who are they that you fear them so?

KOSZAK: It's not them, personally, it's the company, Shill Oil, you know.

DOODLE: Oh dear, once again, art must dirty itself with the

43

sordid commercialists. My dear boy, don't you realize that these big companies, the ones you fear so much, aren't destined to last much longer. But art lasts. The good, the true, the beautiful goes on and on, while these sordid money grabbers will soon be driven from the earth.

KOSZAK: Yeah, I know, but they're due in ten minutes, even less now, and I want to pass 100%. Last month I only got 90% because of the sparkplugs. If I'd had 100% last month, that would have been three perfects in a row and the company would have sent me a scroll with three gold stars. That's what I would have got, if it hadn't been for those gol-darned sparkplugs! Well, I ain't licked yet, no siree! (*Koszak picks up the can of paint and starts for the doorway. Doodle jumps in front of him and places his hand on his bathrobe belt*)

DOODLE: Mr. Koszak, if you begin painting, I'll rip off this bath robe and throw it out in the street.

KOSZAK: Go ahead.

DOODLE: I've nothing under this. I'll be arrested for indecency and you'll be accused of having a place of ill-fame.

KOSZAK: Oh, my God.

DOODLE: How many gold stars do you think your company will give you for that?

KOSZAK: They'll close me out! Look, can't you see it from my point of view. I'm just a hard-working man, trying to make a living. (*At this point, P. Colon Creekbottom enters followed by Martin Luther Huxley. CREEKBOTTOM and HUXLEY are both small, slender, shy men, two peas in a pod*)

DOODLE. Mr. Creekbottom! You've arrived just in time.

CREEKBOTTOM: What's all this commotion. I came right over although I couldn't make heads or tails of what you said on the phone.

ADAMS: Hello, Mr. Creekbottom.

CREEKBOTTOM: Hello, Adams.

HUXLEY: We missed you in church last Sunday, Robert.

ADAMS: Yeah, Reverent Huxley, I got up a little too late.

DOODLE: Mr. Koszak, permit me to introduce you to the president of Kickapoo University, the honorable P. Colon Creekbottom, And, the gentleman accompanying him is the Reverend Martin Luther Huxley, our leading minister.

KOSZAK: Howdy do.

DOODLE: Perhaps never before in your life, Mr. Koszak, have you seen such an assemblage of persons gathered for a cause. At least not in Kickapoo. And this is only a small example of what lies ahead. Why, we have here the only mural in America done by the great Guido Eniro. The world will beat a path to this place. To Kickapoo.

KOSZAK: Yeah, well tell all that to the inspectors.

DOODLE: We fully intend to.

KOSZAK: Good, that's settled. Now, let me begin painting and everything will be O.K. by the time they come and you can talk peaceful like to them.

DOODLE: Oh, no!

CREEKBOTTOM: Look, Doodle, just what is this? I know Guido Eniro was through Kickapoo, left some paintings of some kind, but that's . . .

ADAMS: They're on a wall inside and Mr. Koszak wants to paint them over before the inspectors arrive.

HUXLEY: Surely a little time to consider things, Mr. Koszak.

KOSZAK: There ain't no time left. Business's aren't built by taking extra time for things like this.

HUXLEY: Then they are to be condemned, it seems to me.

KOSZAK: Jees, why couldn't the guy have gone to another station! Oh, if only our plumbing could still have been on the blink! (*There is now the sound of sirens, and all turn to right to watch the entrance of Miss Geraldine Snooker and her lawyer, Eustace Terwilliger. MISS SNOOKER is a chesty gal in her middle fifties. TERWILLIGER is another shy guy. Miss Snooker is dressed in a floweirng lounging robe with gobs of ostrich plumes fluttering about her*)

SNOOKER: Now, just what is this all about?

DOODLE: Miss Snooker!

SNOOKER: (*Announcing herself to others*) Miss Geraldine Snooker.

45

ADAMS: I telephoned her, Mr. Doodle, since she's president of the Ladies Art League.

SNOOKER: And many other leagues too numerous to mention, but enough of that. What is the trouble here?

KOSZAK: Please, let's not go through it all again. Lady, I lease this station from the Shill Oil Company. Part of the lease says I gotta meet monthly inspections and I can't meet inspections if there's stuff on the walls.

SNOOKER: Am I correct in understanding that it was Guido Eniro himself who was here?

KOSZAK: I never heard of him until now, but that's the guy alright. What a jerk! Before we'd had pictures, yeah, but never with signatures underneath.

DOODLE: He signed them.

KOSZAK: Big as life. *Guido Eniro.*

SNOOKER: Imagine. Kickapoo of all places. Finally, after all these years, we have something to be proud of.

DOODLE: What an impetus it will give to our art department.

CREEKBOTTOM: And to our University.

HUXLEY: We'll be known throughout the Christian world. Pilgrimages perhaps coming here to Kickapoo. (*Koszak sneaks the can of paint and starts to enter the Gents room. He is stopped by Doodle*)

KOSZAK: (*Beginning to cry*) You don't understand, none of you. You don't know how close I came to winning that gold star the company gives for three straight 100's in a row. All my life I've wanted something wonderful to happen to me. Some special honor. Well, that's what I can get from Shill Oil. A special gold star. It almost killed me when I didn't get it last month. I'd already bought a little black frame for the scroll. Was gonna put it over my mantlepiece at home. Something for the kids to look up to and make 'em proud of their old man. And now this happens. I'm goosed for good with Shill. Oh, things will seem the same, but they never will again. I'll just go through life without that star, with nothing at all. (*Mr. Huxley comforts Koszak who sits on a box, his head in his hands*)

TERWILLINGER: As a lawyer, I think this thing could be straightened out in some way amicably to all concerned.

KOSZAK. Will you please hurry. They're due here now. I can just feel 'em coming closer and closer and me here and that stuff painted in the back room.

SNOOKER: This place must be enshrined.

CREEKBOTTOM: Enshrined?

SNOOKER: That's the only answer.

ADAMS: How could a service station become a shrine?

SNOOKER: God isn't very particular about where he places his miracles, is he, Reverand Huxley?

HUXLEY: Why ...

SNOOKER: You see, even Reverand Huxley agrees with me. (*Huxley envisions shrine*) Mr. Terwilliger, you have my account book still with you.

TERWILLIGER: Yes, Miss Snooker.

SNOOKER: How much do I still have left in the budget for charities.

TERWILLIGER: (*Consulting*) $4,000. But that's for desperate cases only.

SNOOKER: It seems to me this is a desperate case. Never in the history of our world have people been starving so, starving for art, refinement, culture. Mr. Terwilliger, please inquire to see if this place can be procured.

TERWILLIGER: (*Snapping fingers*) Why, it's been on the market for several weeks now.

SNOOKER: Is that correct, Mr. Koszak?

KOSZAK: Yeah, the company's building a newer, better station on the other side of the street. They left papers here for me in case I found anyone crazy enough to buy.

DOODLE: How much, Mr. Koszak?

KOSZAK: $6,000. It's too much, but these big companies won't come down. They'd rather burn the place and let it rot in the weeds.

CREEKBOTTOM: Burn it down. Oh, my!

SNOOKER: Obviously we are $2,000 short. I shall give my

47

$4,000 with pleasure. It will be the first of the money to go towards the shrine. We'll need someone very dependable in charge. I suggest that I be put in charge. Any objections?

DOODLE: An admirable idea! (*All others agree with great spirit*)

SNOOKER: Thank you very much. This comes as a surprise, heading a national—an international shrine, but I shall try to merit the faith you have placed in me in requesting that I be in charge. Now, about the other $2,000. (*All are silent*)

SNOOKER: Mr. Creekbotom, as I recall Kickapoo U has an emergency fund of $1,000 a year.

CREEKBOTTOM: Why, yes, but . . .

SNOOKER: That will come in nicely.

CREEKBOTTOM: But we usually set it by for the football players who break their legs.

SNOOKER: This year, before each game, you'll have to tell the boys the money for the leg-breaking went for the shrine, and that they'll have to play very carefully with one another.

CREEKBOTTOM: It might be arranged.

SNOOKER: Good, then, that's settled! Mr. Koszak, please bring out the necessary papers.

ADAMS: But there's still a thousand short.

SNOOKER: My dear boy I am aware of that. It's funny I don't remember you, Robert. Such an intelligent face.

ADAMS: Thank you.

SNOOKER: Would you like a great honor bestowed on you?

ADAMS: Anything, Miss Snooker.

SNOOKER: If I liked I could make you the first honorary custodian of the shrine.

ADAMS: Gee!

SNOOKER: It would mean keeping the place clean and without any pay.

ADAMS: Oh, the glory!

SNOOKER: Well, that's settled. Now, about the last thousand.

DOODLE: I would gladly . . .

SNOOKER: Don't disturb yourself, Professor Doodle. We're

48

all familiar with your little extravagances which leave you very little in the bank. (*Turning to Mr. Huxley*) Dear, Reverend Huxley!

HUXLEY: But I have no...

SNOOKER: For twelve years your church has been building a special missionary fund.

HUXLEY: That's true, but...

SNOOKER: For what better purpose than this.

HUXLEY: But what could I tell the Ladies Missionary League?

SNOOKER: The only lady who would give you trouble is Mrs. McGilicuddy.

HUXLEY: That's true.

SNOOKER: For years I've snubbed her publicly. Next week I shall give a party at which she shall be matron of honor. During the party you can tell her about where the $1,000 went.

HUXLEY: I'm afraid...

SNOOKER: Now, gentlemen, the checks, and hurry, for someone's arriving.

KOSZAK: The officials! (*Two non-entities enter bearing the names of Jones and Hargraves*)

JONES: Well, Koszak, ready for inspection.

SNOOKER: (*Stepping forward*) You, sirs, represent the company?

HARGRAVES: Yeah, what's up? Say, what is this? A circus passing through?

SNOOKER: Sir! Mr. Terwilliger, make out my check please and I'll sign. (*To Jones and Hargraves*) Gentlemen, this place has been sold.

JONES: No! Who'd buy this white elephant?

SNOOKER: It was handled entirely by Mr. Koszak here.

HARGRAVES: Koszak sold the place?

SNOOKER: Yes, it's been on fire for a month. It has been on Mr. Koszak's mind, but we demanded that he keep it secret.

JONES: Good old Koszak, didn't know you had it in you.

SNOOKER: This explains, of course, the little matter about

49

the sparkplugs last month, during inspection. I think, in light of this, a certain adjustment might be made.

JONES: Sure, we'll rescind that 90% and make it a hundred for last month.

KOSZAK: You mean ... three in a row.

HARGRAVES: And the scroll with the gold star.

KOSZAK: Whatya know!

JONES: They'll probably put you in charge of the new station across the street too. (*Mr. Terwilliger hands Miss Snooker the check which she signs and hands with the others to Jones and Hargraves*)

HARGRAVES: How'll we make the receipt out, lady?

SNOOKER: To the Guido Eniro Kickapoo Shrine.

HARGRAVES: How's that?

SNOOKER: Just write and we'll explain later. The Guido Eniro Kickapoo Shrine.

ADAMS: Gee, there'll be all kinds of publicity. Even pictures in Life Magazine.

HARGRAVES: Here's your bill of sale, lady. Come on, Jones, let's get out of here before we both discover we've gone buggy! (*Jones and Hargraves leave door right*)

SNOOKER: That's settled! Now, for the paintings! (*Snooker turns to Adams*)

ADAMS: They're in there (*Points to Gents room*) unfortunately.

SNOOKER: H'mm, this presents a problem. (*Koszak stands up smiling*)

KOSZAK: No problem at all, lady. (*Koszak gets on small ladder and takes down Gents sign over door, goes over, takes down Ladies sign off its door, returns, and places Ladies sign over door in question*)

SNOOKER: Indeed, this is a little embarrassing.

HUXLEY: All in the interests of art and culture, Miss Snooker.

SNOOKER: Dear, Reverend Huxley, how right you are. (*Miss Snooker starts for door, stops, and turns*)

SNOOKER: What a historic moment this is. Of course, this

must all be repeated for the newsreels. Oh, if only mother were still alive! (*Miss Snooker turns and enters. There is a deadly silence then a scream by Miss Snooker who comes outside again and faints into the arms of Mr. Doodle who passes her to Adams as he and others rush into room. After a moment they begin to come out*)

ADAMS: What is it. What's the matter.

DOODLE: The paintings . . .

HUXLEY: (*After breathless pause*) They're not religious at all.

CREEKBOTTOM: (*Calling out and beginning to run right*) Mr. Jones, Mr. Hargraves, come back. There's been a mistake . . . a terrible mistake!

Quick Curtain

THE COMPETITOR

All rights, including professional, amateur, motion pictures, recitation, public reading, radio broadcasting, television, and the rights of translation into foreign languages are strictly reserved. All inquiries are to be directed to Crane Johnson, in care of Theatre Press, 550 Fifth Avenue, New York, New York 10036.

THE COMPETITOR

CHARACTERS

KURT JOHANSON, a writer in his mid forties
JOHN MARTIN, a youth in his late teens

Setting: Apartment room, Torquay, Devon, England

Time: The present

THE COMPETITOR

(The scene is the apartment room of Kurt Johanson at Tor-quay, Devon. When the scene opens Kurt is typing at a table, his back to the audience. After a moment John bursts into the room. Kurt looks up at him in surprise)

JOHN: I'm sorry, Mr. Johanson, to burst in on you like this, but it's a matter of some urgency. *(Kurt looks at John with interest)*

JOHN: At least a matter of urgency for me. *(Kurt spins the sheet of paper out of his typewriter and puts it on a pile of other typewritten sheets)*

JOHN: It's about Genevieve. *(Kurt looks again at John, then gets up and goes over to drinks table. John, some of his steam gone, sits in a chair and talks while Kurt fixes a drink for them both)*

JOHN: *(Angrily)* It's unfair, that's what it is. An old man—that's what you are, sir. At least forty-five. It's not natural that a young girl should be attracted to you. Unnatural and unfair. *(Kurt stops his fixing of the drink for a moment and looks at John)*

JOHN: The summer had been going so nicely. I managed to get rid of all the other competition—and oh, sir, there was a lot. Genevieve is a real beauty. Nice family, and all that. And I was in the home stretch, you might say, until you came along. And now, she has eyes only for you. You could be her father—even her grandfather, maybe. It isn't fair. *(Kurt takes the drink over to John and he takes it. Kurt takes a seat opposite John and begins to sip his drink)*

JOHN: Tomorow she and her folks go back to London. And tonight at the party I know she expects you to make advances. She's all ready to sacrifice herself to you. To the great Kurt Johanson—novelist and playwright. Why don't you find a girl your own age. What chance has an ordinary fellow have against you. If it weren't for you—the competition—I'd still be number one. Tonight and on after ... Her folks like me. (*Kurt sips his drink*)

JOHN: I love Genevieve, Mr. Johanson. Truly I do. Everything was going so well . . . until you came. Oh, it isn't your fault. You practically ignored her at first ... almost seemed to force yourself to be polite. Perhaps that's the secret. *Your* secret at least. Pretending no interest when all the other men are throwing themselves at her. Perhaps she's been up here alrady? Or is the conquest planned for tonight? (*Dramatically*) And afterwards, will you just toss her aside and forget her? Break her heart? Please, Mr. Johanson, give Genevieve to me. I love her. Truly I do. Don't go to the party tonight. Tonight is the most important night of my life. Genevieve leaves tomorrow ... (*Kurt rises, walks slowly over to John, takes his drink and puts it on a nearby table. John rises slowly and looks toward Kurt*)

JOHN: Please, sir, don't go to the party tonight. (*Kurt crosses slowly, stops in front of John, takes his hand slowly, holds it for a moment, and then bends over gently and kisses John on the cheek. John doesn't react for a moment, but then begins to beam*)

JOHN: Then you don't like Genevieve. (*Kurt shakes his head and smiles*)

JOHN: It's me you like! (*Kurt nods and smiles*)

JOHN: Yipee! (*He jumps in the air and does almost a somersault over a divan*)

JOHN: And at the party tonight nothing will happen? (*Kurt smiles and shakes his head*)

JOHN: Oh, this is wonderful! (*John runs toward the door and then stops*)

JOHN: You're staying on for awhile, Mr. Johanson, aren't you? (*Kurt nods*)

JOHN: So am I, for awhile. I've read all your books. I like them. All. And you're fun to talk with. To be with. I'll come, visit you if you like. (*Kurt nods*)

JOHN: I'd like a friend, someone older. To talk to. And perhaps we can swim together. There's a beach I know—in a cove—no one ever goes there. No need to wear anything at all . . . perhaps we can go there . . . together. (*Kurt nods*)

JOHN: Tomorrow? (*Kurt smiles and nods. John starts for the door and turns to Kurt*)

JOHN: Thanks, Kurt, thanks very much. (*The two look at one another and John leaves while Kurt looks after him. The curtains close*)

END

THE WOMAN WHO KNEW
PANCHO VILLA

All rights, including professional, amateur, motion pictures, recitation, public reading, radio broadcasting, television, and the rights of translation into foreign languages are strictly reserved. All inquiries are to be directed to Crane Johnson, in care of Theatre Press, 550 Fifth Avenue, New York, New York 10036.

THE WOMAN WHO KNEW PANCHO VILLA

CHARACTERS

EVANGELINE LONGSTREET SMITHERS, a fat slob of a
woman in her seventies
CARLOTTA, her Mexican maid
MRS. SHARPSTREET, a divorcee who lives by her wits
MRS. LOSCHE, a dreary matron from New Jersey
JANET LOSCHE, her buck-teethed, pig-eyed daughter

Setting: Mexico City

Time: Past or present

THE WOMAN WHO KNEW
PANCHO VILLA

(As the scene opens we see an interior of Evangeline's home in Mexico City. Mrs. Sharpstreet is sitting in chair down right trying to contain her boredom at seeing the old routine again. Downstage left on settee are sitting Mrs. Losche and Janet, listening entranced to the dramatic renditions of Evangeline who stands between Mrs. Sharpstreet and the Losche couple, but a little upstage. She is dressed in a Japanese kimona and is grasping a book ecstatically as she speaks)

EVANGELINE: And I was the only one Villa trusted. I, Evangeline Longstreet Smithers. A girl in her twenties, blonde and still a virgin. Only I did he trust. Only I did Pancho Villa trust. Captured in a raid by one of his men—was it Lopez or Fierro? Carried off with the other women. Villa fancied me. I was to be his. But I was brave as I stood before him. Blonde with my young ripe breasts *(Cups breasts with hands)* He liked, Villa liked young full breasts. I was brave and I said 'Senor Villa. Remember I am some man's little sister.' And he spared me. I remained a virgin. There, high in the Sierra Madres, with hundreds of his men swarming about, I remained a virgin. Pancho Villa made history and I, Evangeline Longstreet Smithers, made history along with him. Alone, blonde, and a virgin in my twenties, amongst all those men, but he respected my purity—they all respected my purity—all those women-hungry men groaning with their desire for me. Yes, Villa made history and I made history along with him. All so secret. Such secret history until my book. My great, glorious book. Written so that all may know, all who are alive, and all the generations who are to follow, may know the great history, the great truth. About Evangeline Longstreet Smithers and Pancho Villa there in the mountains. How he respected my youth, my innocence, my virginity. (*All during this scene Mrs. Losche and her daughter sit entranced, gasping at the proper intervals. They are suckers Mrs. Sharpstreet has picked up and brought to Mrs. Smithers*)

MRS. LOSCHE: (*To Mrs. Sharpstreet*) I'm certainly going to review my Mexican history when I get back home to New Jersey.

JANET: (*Adenoidly*) We studied Mexican history in school, but not much about Pancho Villa.

EVANGELINE: Here! (*Grasping book*) Only here is the history written. Here! Here! Here! In my glorious book. The personal intimate story of Pancho Villa. Born Doroteo Arango. That was his real name. *Doroteo Arango*. Born a *peon* who lived on *tortillas y frijoles*. He loved women and horses. I can still remember him galloping toward me there in the *pinos* of the Sierra Madre. On his stallion *Siete Leguas*. Villa was called *El Centauro del Norte*. And I was alone with him. It may be difficult to believe. Up in the rocks and the *mesquite*. Alone. All those men. My virginity. But I was respected. My innocence was respected.

MRS. LOSCHE: And what was the book entitled?

EVANGELINE: (*Half-angrily*) *My Life With Pancho Villa*. All about the revolution. My virginity respected. My waist was slim then and my breasts full and firm. Just as now. (*She pushes up her sagging breasts*)

JANET: When was it published? (*Evangeline is shocked and angry. What has time to do with such things*)

MRS. SHARPSTREET: I believe in 1933.

EVANGELINE: There are certain things that are timeless. I ... my book ... Pancho Villa ... Timeless ... All. His younger sister whom he loved ... ravished by the son of the grand *Don* of the hacienda. Villa, of course, killed him ... an act of honor ... and was forced to flee to the mountains—forced to join the mountain *banditos*. After that ... Chihuahua. Juarez. Ojinaga. (*Mrs. Losche begins to rise*)

MRS. LOSCHE: I'm so sorry, but we must leave, My husband is expecting me at five. And you know how husbands are! (*Janet rises rather stupidly and stands beside her mother*)

MRS. SHARPSTREET: Perhaps, Mrs. Losche, you'd like a copy of Mrs. Smithers' book. (*Janet's bovine face lights up*)

MRS. LOSCHE: Our suitcases are so full, I'm afraid.

EVANGELINE: (*Angrily*) Villa also sang. Sang accompanying himself on his guitar. His favorite was "La Cucaracha." (*Evangeline sings, almost desperately, parading about room and snapping fingers as castenets. It is a pathetic sight*)

EVANGELINE: (*Singing in high cracked voice*)
"La cucaracha, la cucaracha.
Ya no puede caminar;
Porque no tiene, porque no tiene,
Marijuana que fumar."

(*At the end of the song Evangeline turns almost pleadingly to Mrs. Losche*)

MRS. SHARPSTREET: (*Aggressively*) Having Mrs. Smithers' book would be a great souvenir of your trip to Mexico.

JANET: (*Clapping her stubby hands*) Oh, please, mummy, please. (*To Mrs. Smithers*) You're the only famous person I've ever met. You see I'm from New Jersey. (*Evangeline looks at the girl and controls an urge to vomit*)

MRS. SHARPSTREET: Perhaps, Evangeline, you have a copy? (*Evangeline rings a bell and Carlotta shuffles in*)

EVANGELINE: (*Grandly*) Carlotta, bring in a copy of my book. (*Carlotta, not impressed, shuffles off*)

MRS. LOSCHE: How fortunate it was meeting Mrs. Sharpstreet at the tourist office. And how nice it was of her to arrange for us to meet you. I know Janet will include you in her report on Mexico. (*Evangeline looks at Janet again and is almost unable to control her feeling of revulsion of Janet and being "included" in a report. Carlotta returns with the book which she hands to Evangeline. The reverence with which Evangeline takes the book is in contrast to the way it is handed to Evangeline by Carlotta. Evangeline starts to hand it to Mrs. Losche, but then stops*)

64

EVANGELINE: (*Coyly*) If you like, I'll autograph it. (*Janet's face lights up with a moronic expression of delight*)

JANET: Oh, yes! (*Turning to Mrs. Losche*) Mummy! Mummy!

EVANGELINE: (*Rather grandly*) Carlotta, if you'll bring me my pen. *La pluma.* (*Carlotta in her animal way walks over to a desk and shuffles back with the pen. Evangeline takes the pen, opens the book to the title page and signs grandly*)

EVANGELINE: Evangeline Longstreet Smithers. There! (*Evangeline hands the book to Mrs. Losche*)

EVANGELINE: The book sells for 100 pesos in the shops. But you have, in addition, the signature. The signature of Evangeline Longstreet Smithers. Who knew Pancho Villa. Whose virginity remained intact.

MRS. LOSCHE: (*Confused*) I . . .

MRS. SHARPSTREET: (*Coming in for the kill*) I'm certain Mrs. Losche knows the honor she has received in having you autograph the book. If she had purchased the book in a shop there would have been no signature.

MRS. LOSCHE: (*Confused*) I . . .

MRS. SHARPSTREET: (*Sweetly*) The hundred pesos, Mrs. Losche. (*Mrs. Losche opens her purse and hands the bills to Evangeline who almost cannot contain her greediness*)

EVANGELINE: And when you get back to this place where you live . . . where was it?

JANET: New Jersey.

EVANGELINE: Tell them you met Evangeline Longstreet Smithers. Captured by Pancho Villa. But who remained a virgin. Now goodbye. It was nice that Mrs. Sharpstreet brought you. Carlotta, show my guests to the door. (*Carlotta motions to the Americans to follow her and shuffles out. Near the door, unseen by Mrs. Losche and daughter, Mrs. Sharpstreet turns and coldly puts out her hand. Evangeline begrudgingly takes one of the bills given her by Mrs. Losche and hands it to Mrs. Sharpstreet who quickly pockets it*)

EVANGELINE: (*Grandly*) Don't forget, back in your New Jersey, to tell them that Evangeline Longstreet Smithers remained a virgin. In the *pinos* of the Sierra Madre. (*Almost wildly with an arm flung into the air*) With Pancho Villa, I remained a virgin! (*With this note of triumph, the curtain quickly falls as the three women are led out of the room by Carlotta*)

END

THE BIRTHDAY PARTY

All rights, including professional, amateur, motion pictures, recitation, public reading, radio broadcasting, television, and the rights of translation into foreign languages are strictly reserved. All inquiries are to be directed to Crane Johnson, in care of Theatre Press, 550 Fifth Avenue, New York, New York 10036.

THE BIRTHDAY PARTY

CHARACTERS

DEBBY
SANDRA
MARIJANE

Setting: Floor area

Time: The present

THE BIRTHDAY PARTY

(As the scene opens we see two twelve-year-old girls sitting on the floor playing "Jacks." They are Debby and Sandra. After a moment Marijane, another twelve-year-old, enters excitedly with note pad and pencil in hand)

MARIJANE: Mother says I may have the party! Isn't that wonderful! *(Both girls nod without looking up and continue their game)*

MARIJANE: But I can only have twenty-five. No more. I've brought a pad and pencil for the list. *(Both girls continue their game while Marijane sits on floor near them, pad resting on one knee and pencil in other hand)*

MARIJANE: I just love birthdays! Now, for the list! *(Long pause)* I certainly won't invite Gwendolyn. All she does is laugh in that silly way at everything any boy says, even when it's not funny. *(Marijane writes down name)*

DEBBY: Last year her mother gave her two dollars to buy a present for *my* birthday party and she only spent a dollar and kept the other for herself. *(Both girls continue their playing of "Jacks.")*

MARIJANE: And I won't invite Agnes. *(Writing down name)* She took the seat I wanted in class. She knows I like sitting in front by the window.

SANDRA: Her mother drinks by herself. Secretly. All the time.

MARIJANE: And we won't have Helen. *(Writing name)* Do you remember what she gave me last year?

DEBBY: Her mother baked it.

MARIJANE: If I wanted something baked for my birthday, I'd ask my own mother to bake it!

MARIJANE: And Clara won't be invited *(Writing name)* She's always running errands for Miss Wringer when she knows

70

Miss Wringer is my special friend and likes me more than her. And Elsie (*Writing name*) spoils every party the way she ignores the girls and plays only with the boys.

SANDRA: Boy crazy!

MARIJANE: And Susan won't be invited. (*Writing name*) She found that dirty old ragged handkerchief on the floor and in front of everyone, simply everyone, asked me if *I'd* dropped it.

DEBBY: She's so spiteful! (*The girls continue with their game while Marijane pauses for a moment with the rubber end of pencil between her lips*)

MARIJANE: Now, let's see, who else?

SANDRA: (*After pause*) Ernestine. Don't invite Ernestine. (*Marijane adds name to list*)

SANDRA: All she cares about is Billy Rogers and his silly baseball team.

DEBBY: And Grace! Don't invite Grace. (*Marijane adds name to list*)

DEBBY: I'm sure she took my box of crayons.

SANDRA: There's no proof. I think Marjorie took your crayons.

DEBBY: And Marjorie, don't invite Marjorie. (*Marijane adds name to list*)

SANDRA: And Virginia. She telephones Bobby Tyler every night pretending to help him with his homework. (*Marijane adds name to list*)

DEBBY: And Hazel. She kicked me in the vollyball game.

SANDRA: It was an accident.

DEBBY: She kicked me. Lots of girls saw her. (*Marijane adds name to list. Again there is a pause*)

MARIJANE: And Catherine. (*Writing name*) She knows Roger always carries my books from study hall to science. But on Tuesday she pretended her arm hurt and he carried hers instead.

DEBBY: She's so spiteful!

SANDRA: You said Susan was spiteful.

DEBBY: They're both spiteful! (*Both girls continue their*

playing. Again there is a long pause. Marijane puts the rubber end of the pencil again to her lips)

MARIJANE: Now, who shall we *invite*. (*There is again a long pause. Both girls continue their playing. Marijane puts down her pad and pencil on the floor and joins the other girls at the game)*

MARIJANE: Oh, we can decide *that* tomorrow. (*Picking up rubber ball)* I just love planning parties, don't you? (*She throws the jacks and begins playing the game as the other girls look on intently)*

END

THE IMPOSTERS

All rights, including professional, amateur, motion pictures, recitation, public reading, radio broadcasting, television, and the rights of translation into foreign languages are strictly reserved. All inquiries are to be directed to Crane Johnson, in care of Theatre Press, 550 Fifth Avenue, New York, New York 10036.

THE IMPOSTERS

CHARACTERS

COUNT LEONARDO DI FIRENZI
LEOPOLD
JOHN MALCOMB

Setting: Venice

Time: 1910

THE IMPOSTERS

(*The scene is a salon room in the Venetian palace of Count Leonardo di Firenzi. After a moment Leopold enters followed by John Malcomb. Leopold is a very old man, white-haired, and walks with a stoop but with great dignity. John is in his early thirties, dark and good-looking*)

LEOPOLD: We will wait here, Mr. Malcomb. The Count will meet us in this room.

JOHN: (*Looking around*) A real palace! A real palace. And only a month ago I was bartending in Chicago!

LEOPOLD: (*Designating a chair*) Sit there, Mr. Malcomb. (*John sits in chair and continues looking around the room in amazement*)

JOHN: All those rooms! All those rooms we went through to get here. Thirty? Forty? And all that furniture!

LEOPOLD: Treasures collected by the di Firenzi family for hundreds of years.

JOHN: And to think there's a possibility it may someday all be mine.

LEOPOLD: *Yours* if you play your role carefully and do not forget a single item of your story.

JOHN: It's all like a dream. All like a fantastic dream.

LEOPOLD: The moment has arrived, Mr. Malcomb. That moment when all our work is to end in success.

JOHN: Or failure.

LEOPOLD: (*Sharply*) Do not speak of failure. Or even think of it. *You are his nephew.* Never forget it.

JOHN: I sometimes forget the truth and almost believe it myself.

LEOPOLD: The truth and the only truth you must remember is that when the count dies you will be a very rich man.

JOHN: If he doesn't discover I'm an imposter. (*Quickly*) Oh,

76

I realize you don't like the word. But that's what we are. Both of us. Imposters.

LEOPOLD: The Count has no heirs. There is no reason all the money in trust should go to strangers upon his death. No reason why you, who possibly might *really* be his nephew... (*John laughs*)

LEOPOLD: No reason why *I* who have served him loyally for forty years should not also benefit in some way after his death.

JOHN: You'll get your share of the estate. Never worry.

LEOPOLD: I do not worry about that. A prison is not a pleasant place.

JOHN: It's all so fantastic. Like something out of a story-book. Your tracking me down—in Chicago—through the orphanage—helping me to memorize everything I'm to say—and bringing me here. All the work. All the preparation.

LEOPOLD: The stakes are high. One of the greatest fortunes in Venice.

JOHN: And why can't he get it? That's what I don't understand.

LEOPOLD: It's all in a trust fund. To be distributed upon his death to his heirs, and if none, to strangers.

JOHN: And you think he doesn't suspect. Doesn't wonder why you were in America so long?

LEOPOLD: I am merely a servant. I told him it was necessary for me to travel to America for a number of months.

JOHN: He sounds smart. I was never any good at lying. I'll bet he traps me in some way. Throws me out. May throw you out too. Perhaps have us both arrested.

LEOPOLD: No, he would not have us arrested. Never fear.

JOHN: Why didn't he ever marry? Have children?

LEOPOLD: Shh: I hear someone coming. (*The Count enters the salon. He is also elderly, very handsome, and holds himself with great dignity. There seems to be a resemblance between him and the young man. Both men stand as he enters*)

COUNT: (*Looking at John*) So, Leopold, this is the young

man who claims to be my nephew. (*Leopold nods slowly. There is a moment of tension and suspense*)

COUNT: (*To John*) Sit down. (*John reseats himself and the Count seats himself. Leopold stands near the Count's chair*)

COUNT: (*Very coldly*) Leopold has told me of this what he considers to be a great discovery. Upon chance information that a child, possibly that belonging to my sister who fled to America with her lover, had been left with an orphanage after its mother had been found dead. Dead and unidentified. And that upon the wrist of the infant was securely attached a silver medallion upon which was the seal of my house.

JOHN: (*Very simply*) I vouch for nothing, sir, except for the fact that I was left at the orphanage as a baby and was raised there.

COUNT: And the silver medallion.

JOHN: (*After a pause and said a little stumblingly*) It was given to me when I left the orphanage.

COUNT: (*Angrily*) And you thought so little of it you quickly left it at a pawn shop. Where Leopold chanced to see it and began the investigation which brings you here.

JOHN: (*Slowly*) I needed the money.

COUNT: American detectives have furnished me with a very complete file on you.

JOHN: I would have answered any question truthfully and directly. You could have saved money.

COUNT: Log-rolling in Oregon. Cow-punching in Texas. Gold mining in Alaska. Bartending in Chicago. Never at any job for very long.

JOHN: (*Sincerely*) I was searching.

COUNT: For what.

JOHN: (*Simply*) For myself perhaps.

COUNT: (*After a pause*) Who is assisting you in this fraud?

JOHN: (*Stumblingly*) No one.

COUNT: There are many who know of my situation. Know of the great fortune that would come to anyone proving a relationship. But, my dear boy, there will be nothing, nothing, do you understand, unless and until I acknowledge... until I acknowledge... Let the money go to strangers!

JOHN: (*Simply*) Mr. Leopold came to my rooming house one night, knocked on the door, and asked if I would go with him to Venice. Then he told me of the possibility. I know nothing more than that. (*A little angrily*) And I remind you, sir, that it is upon *your* invitation that I have come.

COUNT: (*Quickly*) You speak as an aristocrat! (*Suspiciously*) How so when your only background is an orphanage and vagabondage.

JOHN: I do not know of my parentage. Perhaps it *is* true that my blood is noble.

COUNT: (*Muttering*) The medallion. The silver medallion.

JOHN: It was a carelessly run orphanage. It might have been attached to the arm of another.

COUNT: You are arrogant!

JOHN: And you, sir, most impolite. (*Rising*) I've enjoyed the trip. I've seen Venice.

COUNT: Sit down! (*John sits*)

COUNT: Do you like the palace?

JOHN: I'm overwhelmed.

COUNT: Do you see yourself living here? After my death.

JOHN: I think it would be lonely.

COUNT: Yes, lonely, very lonely... but I suppose you would have women. Many women.

JOHN: (*Shrugging*) It's in my blood.

COUNT: It was in my blood also, but one changes. You have my sister's coloring. Oh, Mr. Malcomb, it would be most tempting to claim you as my nephew, to claim anyone in fact. To have the line continue. Or seem to continue. We have been a noble family. A noble family. We have been artists, and collectors of art, and lovers... and lovers. You have my sister's coloring. It takes a great deal of money to maintain a palace, Mr. Malcomb, more than I've had. You've no doubt noticed the state of disrepair. But, you will have the capital... that is, if I pronounce you my nephew. Leopold assures me that all papers are in order and beyond reproach. My sister's marriage certificate, certificate of birth of child, my sister's death certificate, documents concerning the mysterious disappearance of the child and almost simultaneous arrival of yourself at the orphanage. With the silver medallion. There will be no question here in Venice if I accept. The palace needs work. A great deal of work. Even now you could help.

JOHN: Help. How?

COUNT: If I were to acknowledge our relationship, you could borrow against your inheritance. Borrow a great deal. If some of that could be used now, instead of after my death.

JOHN: I do not know if you are my uncle. I do not claim to be your nephew. But if you believe I am, and if it is possible for me to get any money in advance, I shall give it to you—for the palace or for whatever you wish.

COUNT: Do you mean that? Do you really mean that, Mr. Malcomb?

JOHN: Yes.

COUNT: (*Rising*) You could obtain half.

JOHN: (*Rising*) It will all be yours.

COUNT: (*Slowly*) You have my sister's coloring. And my father's eyes. And you are proud. And you are arrogant. (*Count steps slowly toward John and takes his hand. Then he turns to Leopold*) You may take Mr. Malcomb away now. I have doubts and they are many, Mr. Malcomb, but tomorrow morning at the appropriate place, I shall publicly acknowledge our relationship. Leopold will make the arrangements. (*Leopold, almost unable to betray his happiness, escorts John out of the room. The Count goes slowly over to a table and pours some wine into a glass. He then pours wine into a second glass. When Leopold returns, he hands the second glass to him. They both drink*)

LEOPOLD: (*Quietly*) To our victory.

COUNT: To our victory. (*They both go over and sit down and sip their wine slowly*)

COUNT: I shall finally be able to pay back all you've loaned me.

LEOPOLD: My pleasure.

COUNT: And the palace shall be repaired. *Your idea has*

worked! The palace of di Firenzi. Made dazzling again. I cannot thank you enough, dear friend. (*Thoughtfully*) You know, it's amazing—the family resemblance. And the story is all true, Leopold, all true except for the medallion which you gave him. The resemblance. Did you notice, Leopold, the striking resemblance.

LEOPOLD: It will be noted by everyone. There will be no one who'll question.

COUNT: And there will be money again. Once again the palace will shine. The old glory restored. When I die and he inherits all . . .

LEOPOLD: I shall receive a quarter of what is left. That is our secret agreement.

COUNT: It has worked out very well, Leopold. (*Drinking again*) And you know, Leopold, my friend, it is possible that he *is* my nephew.

LEOPOLD: Yes, it is possible.

(*Both men think and remain silent as the curtains close*)

END

THE GENTEEL COFFIN
FROM BOSTON

All rights, including professional, amateur, motion pictures, recitation, public reading, radio broadcasting, television, and the rights of translation into foreign languages are strictly reserved. All inquiries are to be directed to Crane Johnson, in care of Theatre Press, 550 Fifth Avenue, New York, New York 10036.

THE GENTEEL COFFIN
FROM BOSTON

CHARACTERS

EZEKIEL PITTERBOTTOM
CACTUS DAN
WHISKEY PETE

Place: Somewhere in the wild and wooly West

Time: Around 1840

THE GENTEEL COFFIN FROM BOSTON

(The curtains open on a room empty except for some chairs and a long table at the back of the room in front of a large window. On the table is a custom-made coffin with fancy silk linings. The lid is open. Behind the coffin stands Ezekiel Pitterbottom, a tottering old man in his late eighties who has outlived all sensory pleasures. He wears a black suit, a high white collar, and a rose in his lapel. He has just pulled down the blind in front of the window as the play opens and turns to admire the coffin. He runs ancient fingers across the silk and sighs. After a moment there is a noise off left and Cactus Dan enters. Cactus Dan is in his late forties, a tough hombre, and knows it. Mr. Pitterbottom trembles a bit at seeing him, but summons enough courage to speak)

PITTERBOTTOM: Now, Cactus Dan, you see I'm closed. When I pull down that curtain there over the window, that means I'm closed for the day.

CACTUS DAN: Ezekiel Pitterbottom, I've come to see your fancy coffin.

PITTERBOTTOM: You can see it tomorrow, Cactus Dan. From outside the window. It's to be on display from nine 'til four.

CACTUS DAN: I'se got business elsewhere them hours tomorrow.

PITTERBOTTOM: Well, then you'll just have to wait until some other time.

CACTUS DAN: I'm seeing it now, Ezekiel Pitterbottom! *(Cactus Dan pushes the protesting Ezekiel aside and starts towards the coffin)*

PITTERBOTTOM: Now, you go away from here, Cactus Dan. You may scare other folks but not me. And just because I've a bad heart and may depart from this earth at any time, that's no reason to try to frighten me. (*Cactus Dan touches the silk. Pitterbottom gasps, rushes over, and slaps Cactus Dan on the wrist*)

PITTERBOTTOM: Your hands are dirty, Cactus Dan! (*Cactus Dan again pushes Pitterbottom away with a slight touch of his hand*)

CACTUS DAN: All the way from Boston, imagine! On top a stagecoach, a-riding and rocking all that way, way out here to us Western wolk.

PITTERBOTTOM: (*Professionally*) Made by the finest builders of custom coffins in Boston, Massachusetts.

CACTUS DAN: Mighty nice! It'd be a real pleasure to be buried in a coffin like this. Of course, a person'd have to git himself washed up first, so's not to dirty the silk.

PITTERBOTTOM: This coffin's for a genteel corpse, Cactus Dan. Them plank-board coffins in the back room's good enough for most folks hereabouts.

CACTUS DAN: You know, Ezekiel, I got a hankerin' to buy myself this here coffin.

PITTERBOTTOM: It's already been asked for.

CACTUS DAN: (*Quickly*) But not paid for?

PITTERBOTTOM: Well, no . . .

CACTUS DAN: Yep, it's gonna be a real pleasure to lie there. Big enough for two, it is. If I was to go and git me a skinny wife, we could both fit in, real comfortable-like.

PITTERBOTTOM: If the people in Boston knew what kind of trade I had, they'd never have sent me this coffin. I know it. I must have been crazy ordering it like I did, hoping maybe I'd have genteel trade someday. Well, I'm the only genteel trade in this town and I can't afford to buy it for myself.

CACTUS DAN: How'd you come to hear of this coffin of mine?

PITTERBOTTOM: It ain't your coffin! It's been asked for, like I tell ya.

CACTUS DAN: It's to be mine, Ezekiel Pitterbottom.

PITTERBOTTOM: No, it ain't. And as for your question, it belonged to a very wealthy genteel man from Boston who was

87

a-saving it for his burial, but, by mistake, he got drowned in the ocean and they never found his body.

CACTUS DAN: A real pity.

PITTERBOTTOM: Yes, indeed. His family turned it back for half price, although, for sentimental reasons they wanted to keep it.

CACTUS DAN: It sure brings something to this room, gives it an elegance!

PITTERBOTTOM: Well, Cactus Dan, you've seen it. Now, please leave.

CACTUS DAN: I ain't leaving, 'til you say it's mine!

PITTERBOTTOM: It's been promised!

CACTUS DAN: To what critter?

PITTERBOTTOM: Whiskey Pete.

CACTUS DAN: Me wust enemy!

PITTERBOTTOM: He came first, now get out, Cactus Dan, so's I can lock the door.

CACTUS DAN: (*Taking out revolver*) Where is the varmit? I've been wanting to shoot him daid for years and now's my chance.

PITTERBOTTOM: Cactus Dan, you put that gun back where it belongs. I've a weak heart and I'll have no feudin' in my place. It's respectable and the only genteel place left in town. (*There is a sound of someone entering from left. Pitterbottom gasps and runs behind coffin. Whiskey Pete enters, another tough hombre*)

PITTERBOTTOM: (*Weakly*) It's him, Whiskey Pete! (*Cactus Dan crosses right and turns, gun in hand, to meet Whiskey Pete*)

WHISKEY PETE: (*Calling*) Hey, Ezekiel, where be you. I've got the money. (*When Whiskey Pete sees Cactus Dan he starts to draw his gun*)

CACTUS DAN: Draw it and you're a dead un, Whiskey Pete.

WHISKEY PETE: So's it's you, Cactus Dan. I thought I told you not to cross my path again. This town ain't big enough for the two of us.

CACTUS DAN: I came in after my coffin. Now, if you'll leave, I'll be a-takin' it home with me.

WHISKEY PETE: Your coffin!

PITTERBOTTOM: (*To Cactus Dan*) I told you it was ...

CACTUS DAN: Shed up! Like I say, Whiskey Pete, this here's to be my coffin. I ain't thought much about funerals before, but since I seen this genteel coffin, I decided there ain't gonna be no one buried in it but me.

WHISKEY PETE: That's just what *I* decided when I seed it. And I seed it first.

CACTUS DAN: But you ain't paid for it.

WHISKEY PETE: Hev you?

CACTUS DAN: Not yit, but I'm all-a-set too.

WHISKEY PETE: Since we neither of us hev paid for it, by rights it's mine 'cause I saw it fust.

CACTUS DAN: Why didn't you pay for it when you seed it fust?

WHISKEY PETE: I had to go to the bank. At fust they didnt' want to give me the money, but I told 'em if they didn't loan me the cash, there'd be a bank robbery Sat'dy night and somebody might be killed.

PITTERBOTTOM: Whiskey Pete, you stole that money and I'll not take it.

WHISKEY PETE: Sheddup!

PITTERBOTTOM: I won't shut up. I've decided neither of you is to have it. It's a genteel coffin and I won't waste it on the likes of you what ain't genteel. So, you can both get out!

WHISKEY PETE: Ain't genteel!

CACTUS DAN: You sayin' we ain't good enough for this coffin!

PITTERBOTTOM: Now don't you try to frighten me. I've a weak heart. So now, both of you get out. I can wait. I've lots of time. I can wait until somebody genteel comes along a-needing burial. That's when I'll use this here coffin from Boston, and not before!

WHISKEY PETE: Cactus Dan, I think we's being insulted.

CACTUS DAN: It sounds that way.

WHISKEY PETE: Just to show how genteel we is, I knows how we can settle our little differences here. In a gentlemanly way. Like a genteel would do it in Boston.

PITTERBOTTOM: You're up to no good, Whiskey Pete!

CACTUS DAN: What's on your mind, Whiskey Pete?

WHISKEY PETE: We'll have a duel to see which of us gits the coffin. That's the genteel way of settling differences.

PITTERBOTTOM: It's against the law!

WHISKEY PETE: The law ain't come this far west yet.

CACTUS DAN: I'm a-willin' to duel if you are. Name the place and time.

WHISKEY PETE: The place is right here and the time's now!

PITTERBOTTOM: Not here. Not in my place. I won't have dead bodies around!

WHISKEY PETE: Stand out of the way, Ezekiel. Cactus Dan, put your back to mine. We'll walk ten paces, turn and shoot. The one who comes out alive gits the coffin.

CACTUS DAN: What about the dead 'un.

WHISKEY PETE: He gits a plank-board coffin.

CACTUS DAN: Fair enough.

PITTERBOTTOM: I won't sell the coffin to either of you, do you hear, to ...

CACTUS DAN AND WHISKEY PETE: Shuddup! (*The two men line up back to back and begin taking their paces, then turn and shoot. Just before the guns go off, Pitterbottom runs out trying to stop them and falls on his face. Both men are stunned, then walk cautiously forward*)

CACTUS DAN: Whadya know!

WHISKEY PETE: Crazy fool walked right in the line of fire! (*Both men bend down and look at Ezekiel*)

CACTUS DAN. Must have gone in his ears, both shots. Nary a trace of a bullet.

WHISKEY PETE: Nope, nary a trace. (*Both men look at the body for a moment, the slowly turn towards the coffin*)

CACTUS DAN: I wanted that coffin like sin.

WHISKEY PETE: Me, too.

CACTUS DAN: I don't suppose he'd be happy with just a plain wooden plank coffin.

WHISKEY PETE: No, he was always sort of genteel-like. (*After a moment, both men carry the body and place it in the coffin*)

CACTUS DAN: He sorta goes with the coffin, don't he, Pete.

WHISKEY PETE: Yep, it certainly becomes him.

CACTUS DAN: I be needin' a drink.

WHISKEY PETE: Me, too.

CACTUS DAN: I reckon he'll be found in the morning.

WHISKEY PETE: Yeah, I reckon. (*Both men turn to leave. Cactus Dan, however, sees something*)

CACTUS DAN. Wait. (*Cactus Dan goes over and points at something in the wall*)

CACTUS DAN: Whiskey Pete, here's your bullet. (*Whiskey Pete is amazed, but goes to the other side of the room and points to a spot*)

WHISKEY PETE: And here's yours! (*Both men are silent for a moment*)

CACTUS DAN: I guess his end had just come.

WHISKEY PETE: Yip. Right time, too, 'fore he sold the coffin.

CACTUS DAN: Pete, old hombre, you won't let out how I missed you. My eyes ain't so good no more.

WHISKEY PETE: Mine ain't as sharp as they used to be either. I'd appreciate it if you'd keep sort of quiet about my missing you. (*Both men approach and shake hands*)

CACTUS DAN: This calls for a drink, I think. (*Whiskey Pete nods. They begin exiting when suddenly there is the sound of a groan from the coffin. Both men throw themselves into one another's arms*)

WHISKEY PETE: A ghost!

CACTUS DAN: Coming to haunt us! (*Ezekiel pushes himself up dizzily and looks at the men*)

PITTERBOTTOM: You shot and missed one another. That's what! (*Both Cactus Dan and Whiskey Pete rush over*)

CACTUS DAN: On purpose, Ezekiel.

WHISKEY PETE: Sure, Ezekiel, on purpose.

PITTERBOTTOM: The whole territory afraid and you missed one another at ten paces!

CACTUS DAN: We've decided the coffin is to be yours, Ezekiel.

WHISKEY PETE: A present from us.

CACTUS DAN: Each of us paying half.

PITTERBOTTOM: (*Looking around*) It is a fine coffin.

WHISKEY PETE: Most genteel in the territory. (*Both men help Pitterbottom out of the coffin*)

CACTUS DAN: And now, for our drink.

WHISKEY PETE: More than one, Pete, old pal (*They both take Ezekiel arm in arm*) The first one is to us, then one for Ezekiel, and then one for the genteel coffin from Boston! (*They all lift their hands to an imaginary toast to the coffin and skip merrily off the stage as curtains close*)

END